Dogleg brick

You probably know that some walls are built of stone (which is natural) and some are built of bricks (which are man-made), but did you know that walls can be built of almost anything? Look inside to find out about walls made of rubber, wax, metal, glass, wood, ice, and alligators – and see if you can think of any other kinds.

Be careful about climbing on walls, though, whatever they're made of. Remember what happened to Humpty Dumpty!

Plinth squint brick

Limestone sneck

Bevelled bat brick

Half round coping brick

Decorative brick

*For Lucy and Emily*
J.A.
*For Amelia*
A.B.

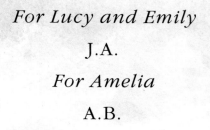

First published 1993
by Walker Books Ltd
87 Vauxhall Walk
London SE11 5HJ

Text © 1993 Judy Allen
Illustrations © 1993 Alan Baron

This book has been typeset in Garamond Light.

Printed and bound by
Colorprint Offset Ltd, Hong Kong

British Library Cataloguing in Publication Data
A catalogue record for this book is available from the British Library.

ISBN 0-7445-2251-X

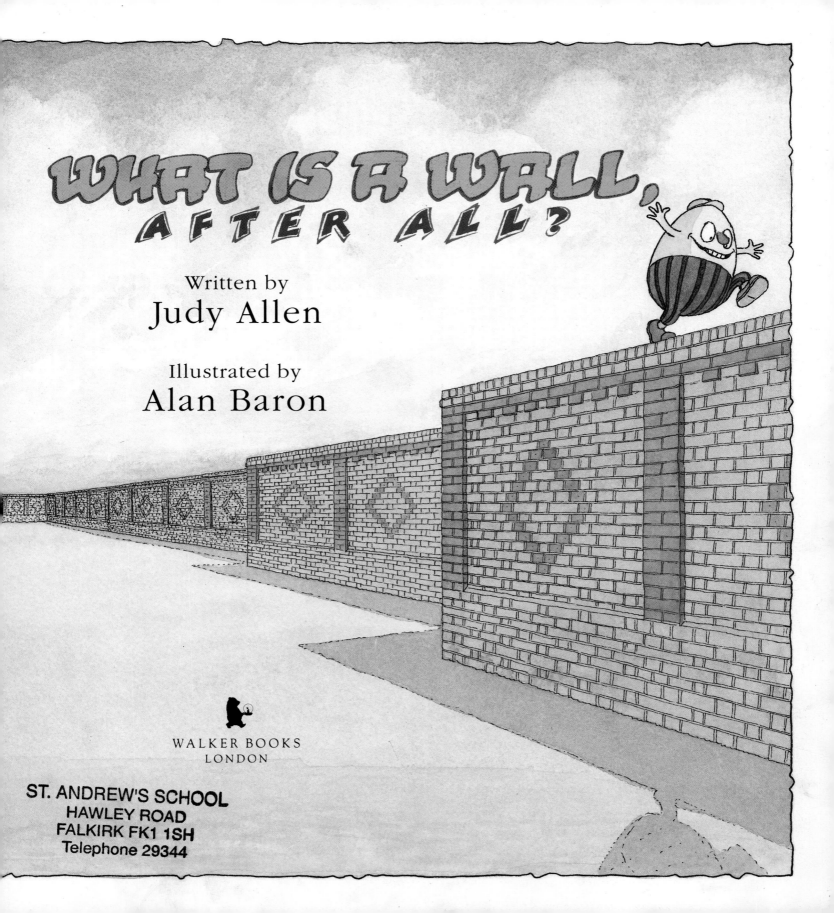

# WHAT IS A WALL, AFTER ALL?

Written by
## Judy Allen

Illustrated by
## Alan Baron

WALKER BOOKS
LONDON

Wherever you are when you open this book,

I bet you can see a wall, if you look.

Could you
build a wall?

No problem
at all!

Put brick
on brick.

Mortar makes
it stick.

It's a weak wall, a sick wall, a leaning-on-a-stick wall,
a feeble wall, a quaky wall, a crumbly, tumbly, shaky wall.

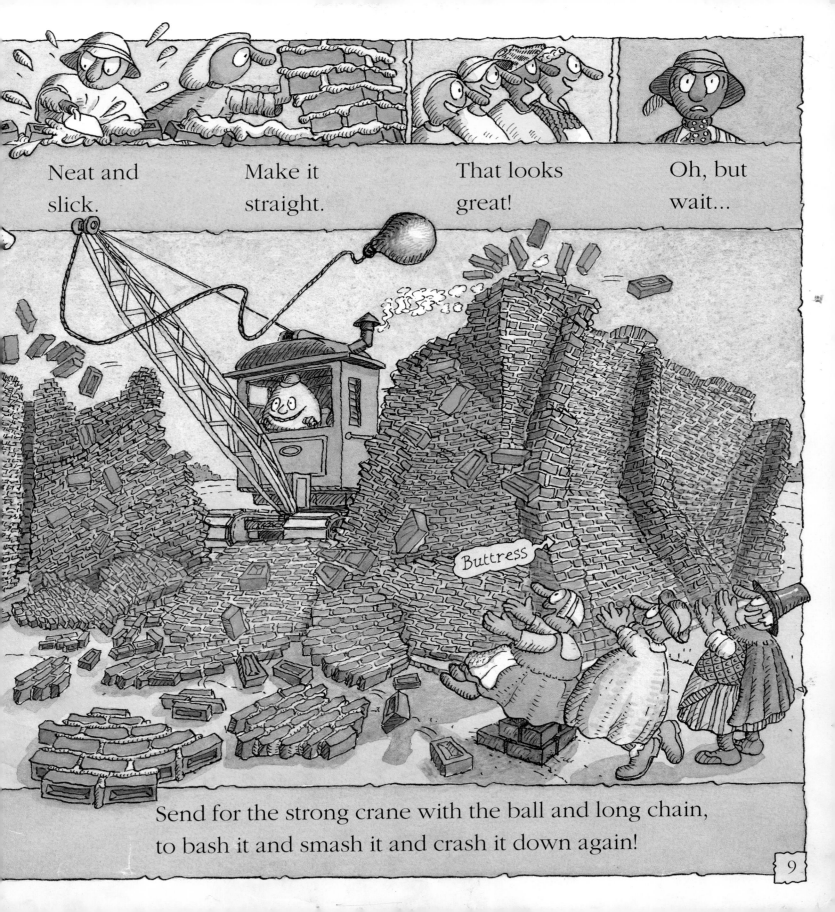

Neat and slick.

Make it straight.

That looks great!

Oh, but wait...

Send for the strong crane with the ball and long chain,
to bash it and smash it and crash it down again!

9

A drystone wall may look like a huddle
of jagged stones, ragged stones, all in a muddle,
a jumble that could easily tumble and fall.
Look carefully, though, it's cleverly done:
each stone is balanced on another one.
Each shape has been picked to fit its own space,
so the wall stands firm on a solid base.

10

The walls of castles are built of blocks –
large blocks, stone blocks, cut out of rocks.
They are nearly square and almost neat
and mortar joins them where they meet.

There are walls made of glass that shine in the sun,
and rubbery walls that are silly – but fun!

There are brick walls and thick walls and walls owned by cats,
and deep underground there are cave walls, with bats.

There

are

tall

walls,

high

walls,

climb

up

to

the

sky

It has to have a light at the top to warn aircraft not to hit it.

walls... and little, low, short walls that creep along the ground.

There are big, long, wide walls, we've-got-something-to-hide walls,
and the walls of a lighthouse that have to be round.

15

There are walls that are horribly fierce,

There are walls that are meant to get hot,

and walls that are terribly old.

and walls that ought to stay cold.

Some walls are there to shut out invaders
(a safe keeps out robbers, a fort keeps out raiders).

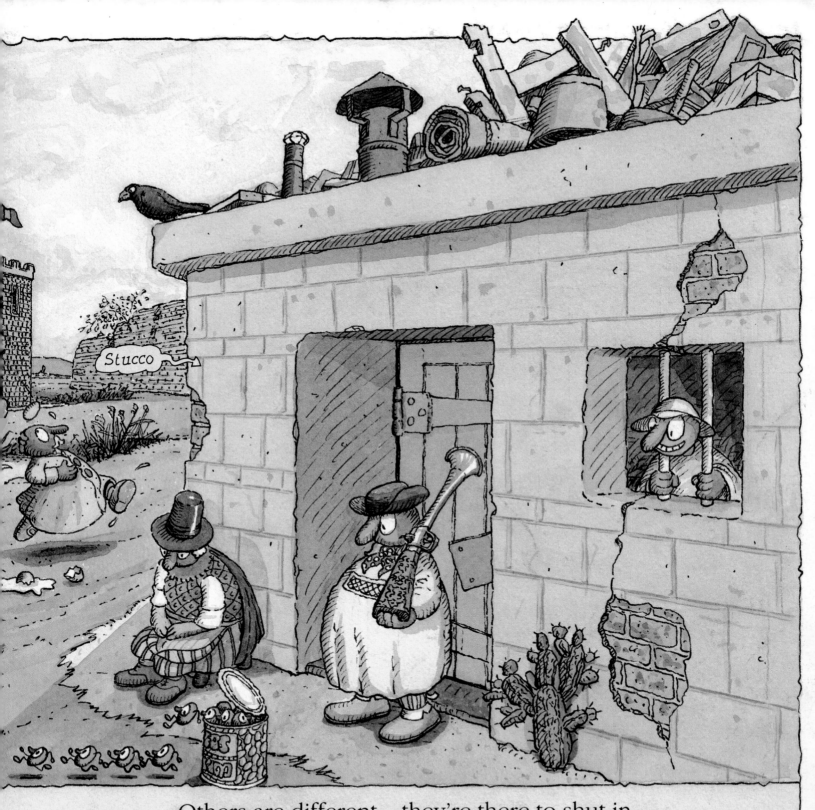

Others are different – they're there to shut in.
(Think of people in prison, or beans in a tin!)

Here is a wall that has to be tough
so it won't collapse when the weather gets rough,

and the wind is wild and the waves pound hard
and the stormy seas try to break through its guard.

Here is a wall that is long, strong and round:
it's the wall of a tunnel that runs underground.

The wall of this dam has to stand like a rock
to hold back the river whose path it must block.

Most indoor walls are plain and flat,

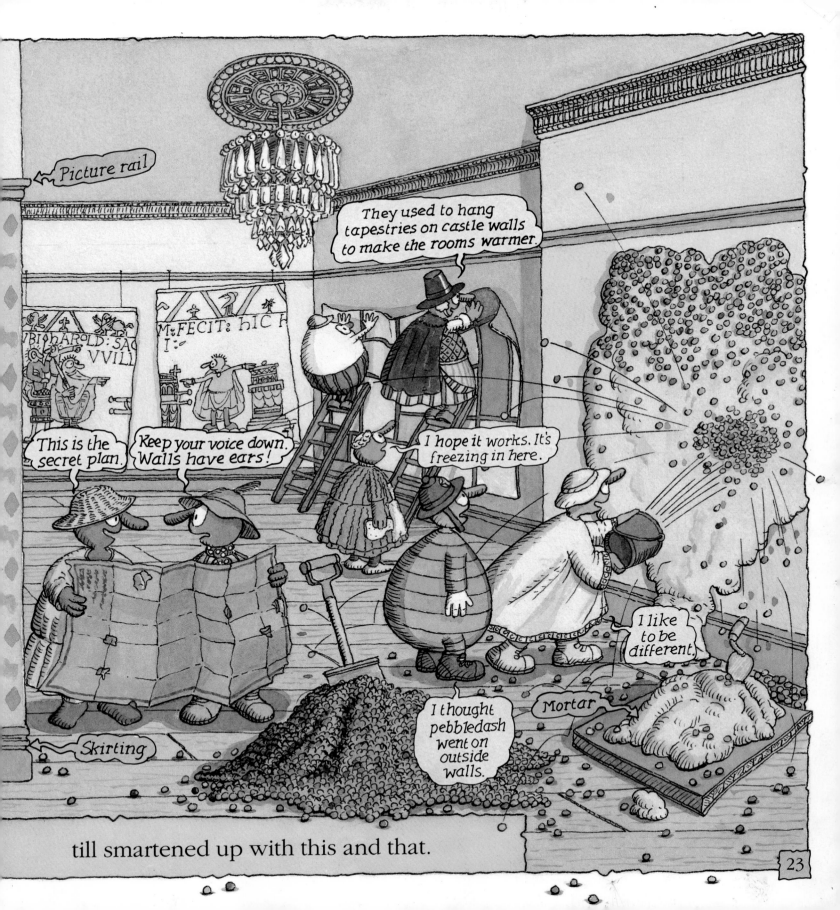

till smartened up with this and that.

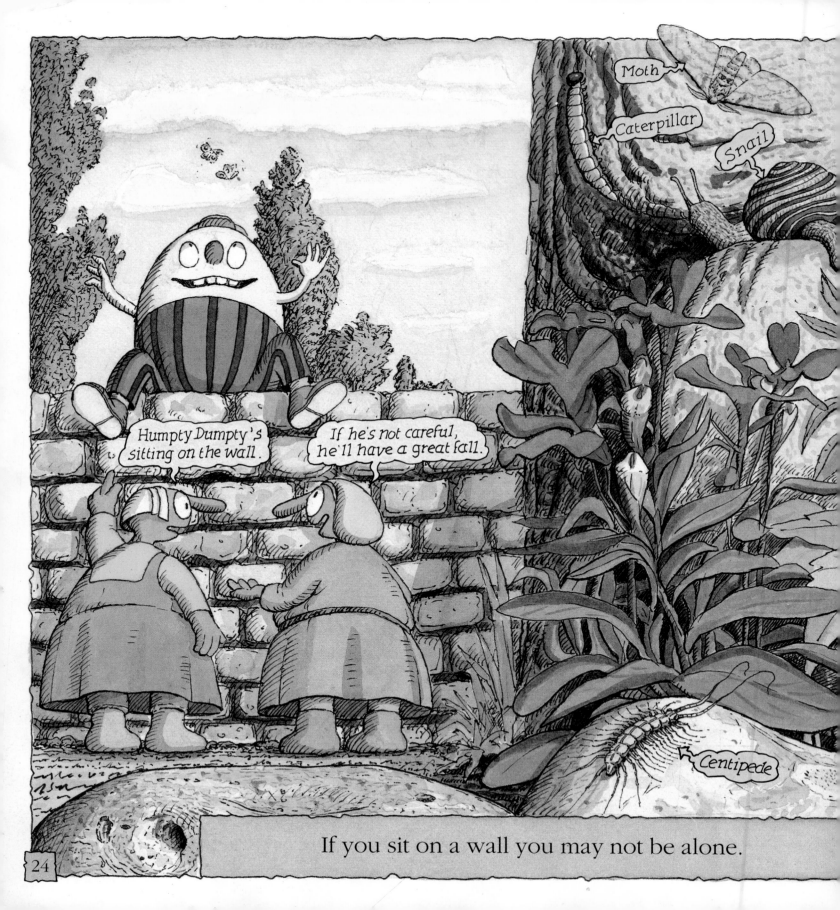

If you sit on a wall you may not be alone.

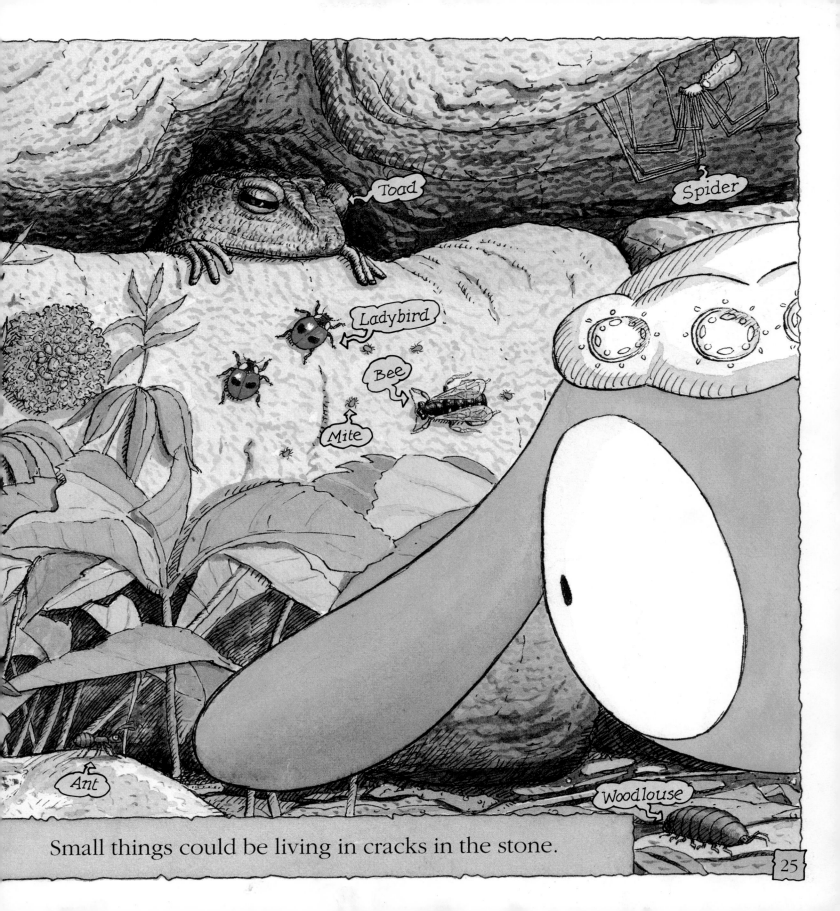

Small things could be living in cracks in the stone.

If you want to climb a mountain wall you will probably need stout boots and crampons and warm clothing and pegs to hammer into narrow cracks and wedges to hammer into wide cracks and a peg hammer to put them in with and an ice axe and a hammer axe (which is a short ice axe) and a strong rope and a hard hat.

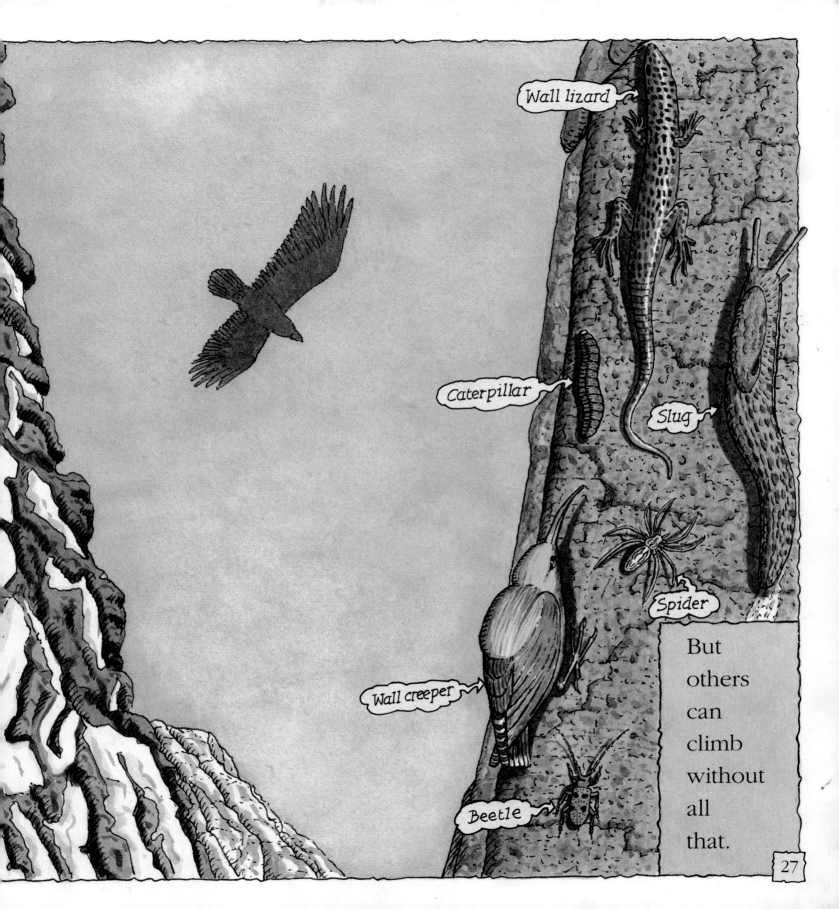

But others can climb without all that.

Where are you? In a room? In a garden? In a car? A bus? A train?

In a field? On a boat? Maybe up in a plane?

In the street? On the beach? In a hot-air balloon?

In a café? In bed? Perhaps on the moon?
Well, wherever you are when you finish this book,
I bet you can see a wall, if you look.

Bevelled bat brick

Half round
coping brick

Decorative
brick

# Index

Look up the pages to find out
about all these walls.
Don't forget to look at
both kinds of words:
this kind
and
*this kind*.

Dogleg brick

Plinth squint brick

Limestone sneck